This book is dedicated to

Mumma

Contents

This image is a reflection of how biases around age can affect both humans and nature. Both the young and old are often overlooked and silenced. The ageism bias needs a challenge as well as an exploration. The poem Sequoia tree is a small attempt at doing so.

1. The Sequoia Tree

(Won Gold award at Queen's Commonwealth Essay Competition'23)

In a large tract of land
Owned by a formidable middle-aged man,
A seed was sown
Near an old Sequoia tree.
The tree stood; stoically
It seemed like an institution agonizing over lost glory
With its gnarled bark, weathered branches and slender trunk
But imbued in that wrinkled exterior
Lay a silent testament to fortitude
A symbol of endurance,
And a majestic yet mature witness to eons of man's victories and defeats.

The seed, in its nascent stage, was youthful and vibrant;
It looked up to the Sequoia tree with fascination and curiosity
The innocent seed, oblivious to worldly ways and propriety,
Looked up and said,
"Respected tree, it seems to me that I need more water than I'm getting.
But other small seeds have told me that I'm too young to even ask.
Does age matter so much?"
The tree smiled at the curious little mind

And replied, "Oh dear, that is a complicated matter,
For throughout the history of mankind
I have seen opportunities denied to the young and old alike."

"In many cultures, the old are viewed as a liability,
Sometimes even a waste of resources and time."

"Like the rivers that are polluted once they are old and large,
And the elderly mountains that are cut for marble and granite;
Those fish that are too big to escape the fishnet, sell for a higher price
And elephants with developed tusks are killed for their precious ivory
Once ripe, fruits end up as a gastronomic delight
My dear comrades, the tigers are hunted down
And skinned to become floor mats for the humans to rest their feet on"

"But dear, the young suffer the shackles of prejudice too.
Their voices deserve to be amplified,
Yet they are not empowered,
And are often abandoned in their state of distress.
Take a look at the lions that kill young cubs to eliminate competition,
Or the reptilian snakes which possess no maternal instinct
And leave their children in this world, with no one but themselves to count on

Or the cuckoo mother who thinks it's smart to trick
other birds into raising its own
And the workplaces that say the youth are too young to
lead or take key decisions"

"In this world, dear seed, closer to the end, even the
heart is nothing more than a mere organ;
And even this wise brain is considered worn out.
It hurts to have been overlooked
For my ambitions in my youth
For my wisdom in my old age
Sadly, we are valued for what's visible or quantifiable.
Age is both!"

"Look around little seed and you will see
Middle aged thorns and bushes receiving water and
manure, aplenty
They are equipped to flourish in this world,
We are mere obstructions,
Easily dispensable,
Often overlooked,
Always misunderstood."

"You, little seed, think about carrying my message
forward
Across rivers and streams
Through every animal that passes by
Maybe one day this message reaches the humans,
Maybe one day they have an epiphany,
Maybe there is a chance to change,
Don't give up little seed,

Try to make your voice heard,
For justice often comes after generations grind through passionate imploration,
Ironically led by the young and the old."

"Question, little seed,
Question the assumptions
Why is it that what the young and old have to offer
Doesn't appeal to mankind?
The young and the old have a lot to give,
If only one knows when to learn, nurture or even forgive
It's the incapability and rigidity of mankind
That manifests into discrimination,
Little seed- ask questions
And the answers, objectively evaluate"

Just then the middle aged and brawny farmer
The planter of the seed, arrived
With a hammer that struck hard
A loud sound was heard that reverberated
And drowned the tree's last words
A scatter of light rays through the falling leaves
Put the spotlight on the darkness of ageism!

The tree which stood 160 feet tall was brought to the ground
It fell close to where the little seed grew
The earth shook just a bit
The seed's conscience shook significantly more
A cry emerged from his soul.
An echo that reminded him to

"Ask questions and evaluate answers."
For now he just had one question;
It wasn't "*does* age matter?"
It was-
"Why *should* age matter?"

Happiness is about living life lightly yet in a deep manner and a complete life is not necessarily a long one. I wrote this poem when as a young person I first confronted death and realised that while death is hard but life, well, it's truly beautiful.

2. The Happiest Man

He climbed rugged mountains, yet never felt the cold,
He knew forever would just be a limited number of days,
So he stayed away from making promises
knowing it would be folly to believe he could keep them,
He led the happiest life in the world.

He valued the weight of every breath,
Understood the association of colours with perception,
So he concluded that goodness was an illusion,
He would not fall prey to such delusion,
Thus he was the happiest man in this world.

He enjoyed his tea even though the teapot served just one cup,
Yet he never sought company,
His greatest conversations were frequent ones with his
conscience,
Immorality never seemed to touch him, so in its presence
he did not flinch,
This made him the happiest man in the world.
So when death approached him, he hugged it graciously,
He measured his life,
not based on years,
For this man, was just a boy.

Righteousness captures the word "right" and from a very young age we, humans, are taught to be right and to do right. Flaws and sins are villainous traits, they are abhorred and rejected yet sins enter all our lives either discreetly or explicitly. This poem captures the authenticity and legitimacy behind the seven sins in an attempt to make it easier for us all to be more accepting of our flaws.

3. Sins and Survival

An indolent child scattered just a few seeds.
Chance, not choice played a part in the birth of the plant,
So its origin stemmed out of *sloth*.
The seed then gnawed the nutrients of the soil,
Its survival thus was incumbent on *gluttony*.
Not satiated perhaps, it drew on light from the sun, water from the skies,
Its succulence was an outcome of *greed*.
The flowers that bedecked the growing plant bestowed it with beauty,
Beauty that translated into its *pride*,
Beauty that attracted insects for procreation,
Nature seemed to have encouraged as well as embraced *lust*.
Yet with beauty that was boundless,
The plant felt so small when it saw the trees around it with intimidating stature,
Its *pride* crumbled to its *envy*.
Years passed on, the stem turned into a bark,
The tree now had it all, beauty built on strength,
Yet one blow of the axe stirred its last sin,
Wrath swept the tree, and in anguish, it fell to the ground.
The tree albeit filled with sins,
Was an altruistic provider too,
Of oxygen, fruits, shelter, and beauty.
Humans are sinners. True.
But they too are graced with virtues aplenty.
Sins add as much to life as they

May take away from character
They make us human,
They make for lessons,
They make us complete.

4. My Titanic

I valued the beauty of the human heart,
But his was the expanse of a never ending sea
But when 'he' measured his heart he subtracted too much worth
Angels don't keep mirrors I reminded myself,
But I wish I could buy him a mirror,
Or be a mirror to him.
Sometimes he smiled through summer
Other times he surrendered to the cold of winter
I stood by him like the sun, through all the seasons
The intensity of my warmth changed
But I was always there.
An iceberg was approaching, I could feel it.

Then came the chatter, the playful smiles
It covered the uncertainty and seas of insecurities
The boat was moving forward, progressing
But I was in the glorious boat silently weeping.
The weeping was a premonition for the crashing with the iceberg
Then came in the pain and the realization that the boat would sink

This Titanic journey is that of the doomed boat of love
It shows hope, even perfection but proves to be Fatal.

One's inner critic can get all too powerful at times, making a person feel trapped within a complex web of dark tangles. I made this sketch to depict the varied dark directions a burdened soul could take until they start to listen to what their loved ones say to them.

5. You say

When my barren land shows cracks
And my petals are marred
When I'm sinking in tributaries of emotions
Distributaries of fear
Sinking, way too far.

When a wave of trouble drowns me under
And an ocean of insecurity takes me over
When my body turns
Into a shriveled, crumbled mold

When everything around me seems
Like a thread between living and leaving
Then you pull the thread to your side
And I finally find myself breathing
You say "Beautiful flower, you are too bright to leave this world"
And so when my barren lands
Feel desolate, fissured
You enter in like a river
And sweep the uneven bumps over

And when I'm drowning
You always tell me
"Beautiful flower
You can survive even in this water."

This painting and the poem are inspired by nature around multiple facets- adaptability, survival and the power of interpretation - of how the same thing can mean different things to different people. I'm sure, much like life, both this art and the poem will be seen in their own unique way by the readers.

6. Nuances of Nature

A chameleon is known to take the color of its surroundings
Blending and fusing itself with all that's around
Is it the only one?
Is it only survival that triggers a camouflage?

Not quite

For look at the rain
It takes the color of our unstated emotions
Look at the drops that fall from the sky
That almost seems to be an ornament to our mood.
While some dance in the rain with glee
Associate it with a glorious harvest
Anticipate the petrichor which fills the air
Others suffering from the shackles of their sorrow
View rain as an aggressive or annoying aberration

Yet rain breaks the monotonous lives we are subjected to
It is a shift from the hustle of the city
It aligns itself with the moods of the people
Like a reminder of the value of perspectives
Like it was meant to be what others wanted it to be
Like it would disappear or be visible
Like it molded itself to appeal to its audience
Much like, just like a chameleon

This poem is a lived experience for so many people I have met. Each one wanting someone else's life but sadly forgetting to value their own. Through this painting and the poem, I encourage everyone to take the journey of self exploration and realise that the world is large enough and amazing only because it has a place for everyone.

7. The Sun and Moon

The sun longs to be like the moon
To grace the night sky with such calm
To be the muse of all the romantic poets
To witness the expansive sky bespangled with stars
To be attractive in a rather conventional way

But equally the moon longs to be the sun
To be magnificent without the company of the stars
To be worshiped by the devotees
To have authority, dominance and prominence
To be scintillating yet daunting

If the sky can be enough to reflect both their light
Why do they fall short
In recognising their own worth?

8. Last (wo)man standing.

My life was a game of chess,
Every move and step was planned.
My pieces were on the board.
Ready to attack.
The pawn - or the smallest part of my life, was my own will.
It seemed really weak, but even this pawn could kill!
Slowly into the game, all my pawns were gone.
I needed another piece to depend on.
As the game proceeded, my knight was removed.
The fastest thing I possessed was my intelligence.
I had planned to use it.
So I took it out, but it got killed.
I still had my rook.
Carefully I took it out.
It was supposed to go fast and knock everything out.
In my life the rook was like my friends.
They cleared the way so I could be safe
But even those friendships came to an end.
I resorted to removing my bishop.
It was protecting my queen all along.
What protected me like this bishop was a nice melody or a song.
It only took a few notes to save me from my worries.
But the bishop too was gone.
Two pawns on my board were all that was left.
A king and queen, side by side.
The king sacrificed itself for the queen that survived .

So then it came to the queen.
Who had zero defense.
When checkmate killed her.
My queen had died.
Let me tell you though
Things are different.
I don't need a king or an army to save my life.
It's high time we stop "protecting" women,
They can save their own lives
Honey, you see the thing is
At the end, the queen was the last to die.

This painting captures a moment and a place. That moment when the finiteness of life gives way to the infinite untouchable world of the beyond. The poem captures the helplessness when losing a loved one and the hope that they are in a better place.

9. The Room of Dreamers

A young man had just said his goodbyes to his only love
He was a tornado and she was the wind
She loved too soft, he spoke too loud
But just how the tornado never follows the wind
He left her and reached the room of dreamers

A young woman collected a bountiful of apples
Anyone who saw her deduced that she was mad
But the apples fed those who couldn't see
Yet it was the common folk who were blind to her compassion
It was no surprise that she too reached the room of dreamers

The man who promised his daughter he would meet her when the clock strikes thirteen
He had showered her with countless streams of joy
Yet there wasn't a single drop of water shed from his eye
He was graced with fountains of water and calm
When he reached the room of dreamers

What a gift of heavenly peace the room of dreamers was
To those who had deceased
Yet kept love, sacrifice and service alive
Even after their sleep silenced their breath

Looks and vanity are such a paramount theme among the generation today. Prejudiced stereotypes, body shaming and insecurities affect so many of us. In my view this happens as more often than not looks are processed and interpreted. Through this poem I hope to invoke the role of emotion and appreciation with respect to looks among humans just the way they are deployed when looking at nature.

10. The Beauty Within and Around

What we feel
When we see
That mauve flower in the backyard garden
We marvel it's beauty, it's color
That maroon flower atop the hill
We marvel it's beauty, it's structure
That marigold flower near the city drain
We marvel it's beauty, it's presence

What we think
When we see
The night sky from a rooftop cafe
We admire its expanse,it's stillness
The morning sky after a prayer in a temple
We admire its purity, it's promise
The predawn sky, while wading through busy roads
We admire its myriad colors, its confusion.

Wonders of the world or parts of nature
Words fail us to describe them aptly
Opinions can never be conclusive
To decide what's better, more picturesque-
The northern lights or the Amazon river
The Great Barrier Reef or Sandunes in Sahara

For when we look at nature
We think that
No size is special
No mass is right
No structure is the norm
No color is better

But
When we see our bodies
We don't feel
We analyze what we see
We don't accept
We scrutinize what we see
We don't appreciate
We stereotype what we see

His creation around us
Leaves us spellbound
But, sadly
His creation of us
Leaves us just bound

Bound to notions, that,
Sizes have norms
Shapes have names
and
Colors indicate stature

Bound to believing that
Individuality is an abnormality
Bound to harboring
Lifelong insecurities
If only we would just "feel"
When we see
Human bodies

11. A Million Times More

An oppressive heat for the world
But light filled with hope for me
You are my sun, my biggest star
I cannot look at you for too long for that would kill me
And it has hurt my eyes before
So I love you from a distance
As we are apart due to forces of the world

Your love is akin to a tumultuous sea
The waves pull me under and suffocate me
My senses surrender and mind collapses
But there always comes a moment
When I defeat the waves, and rise up to catch a glimpse of you
It may seem like a feeble attempt at survival
Yet for me it is a precious breath of life
As I see you shining bright
Soon after though I'm dragged back into the depths of the morbid sea
I surrender, I don't complain
In fact, I feel fulfilled
For in that one moment, I have lived
And loved wholesomely
And for that one moment
I could drown,
Even a million times more

12. Brave are Those

Materialistic desires are quick to fulfill
Like quicksand in the middle of the desert of morality
But when you jump you are roped in
And in your doom you can scream and shout
But it's you who jumped
You who cannot be pulled out

Hardwork is that ocean you have to kayak through
In your devotion, you are fulfilled
Even when you have nothing but a sky
And empty oceans ahead to look into

It is easy to hate, easy to cheat
For hate is our mother tongue
That you and I speak
But rare it is to dream and to feel
To love someone is your greatest gift
Every tear you shed in their name
Is a complement to your heart

It takes courage to declare the love you feel
Courage to devote yourself to a dream
And that is why I have always believed
Love is only for the brave
And hate, for the weak

This painting is of a brave beautiful woman who is willing to embrace the many moods and shades of love. When I think about true and deep love, I think of a person who is truly brave. For being in love is an unsteady, heady walk on a precarious path.

13. To Be In Love

To truly know how it feels to possess a secret
To dance with glee to a song that hasn't even begun
To be thrilled, with just their thought
To find the beauty of all the wonders of this world, dull
When compared to their smile
To willingly jump into a swamp of emotions
And know that in it, lies your destruction
To climb a mountain with high spirits and no sight of its peak
To swim towards depths you cannot even see
To trust destiny, without any glimpse of certainty
To find poetry not in these words
But in touch, presence and emotion
To offer in perpetuity unfeigned dedication
Is to be in love.

The human mind is conditioned into making firm associations. Stereotypes, beliefs, cliches exist across cultures and generations. This poem entails the benefactor of positive associations questioning oft made assumptions. It's a simple conversation with a profound message or perhaps it's profound because it's so simple.

14. The mighty one

"We must exchange goodbyes
For as I was gliding through the skies
I saw a terror I could not digest
A lion with a long mane and powerful forelegs
Strong claws and sharp teeth
With strength that has no parallel"

With fear oozing out of every word
The crow said this and set us animals into a frenzy of fear
The birds began their journey towards the skies
The dismayed elephant let out deep cries
All animals rushed out in different directions
And within a few seconds, the chaos became inaudible

I crept up a tree in a jungle now so empty
For I am a little squirrel, it is easy for me to hide
A lion has an appetite and I'd hardly suffice
I woke up after a few hours
And right beneath the tree
A moribund lion lay
Staring right towards me

"Please do not eat me" I said as a plea
The lion said, "Do not worry dear, I will not feed on thee"
"Oh really" I said, "how do you plan to survive?"
"Life itself is giving up on me, little squirrel
I already know that at this tender age, I am dying

Now this is a fact I thought by now, everyone would know
But, perceptions, you see, are often hard to go

Having said that, I would like to thank you, little squirrel
For not running away from me and staying on to listen to me
For often it takes one
To change the status quo and to break the patterns free.

15. You and I

I was a glass of cold water
Distant, awkward and reserved
And you were gloriously lukewarm
Uncontroversial, comforting and approachable
I always felt that mixing the water of both glasses
Would make me,you and us perfect

But you wanted to steer clear of me
The idea of cold water was a tad appealing
But you wouldn't go all in
Because it would create a sudden change
Or some other inconvenience

My glass of half filled cold water
Was a prepossessing glass, you said
You loved the design, the patterns
The myriad colors, shape and structure

Yet you didn't love the substance it carried
You were too afraid to set foot
Into my world of bold intricacies
I was always either too much or too less,
I desired and required more of you,
But you, didn't need more of me,
I was never enough.

I *am* a glass of half filled cold water,
To you, it might be inadequate and half empty
Yet I feel quite full.

This poem and painting are close to my heart and I turn to these as a reminder quite often. I painted a stunning warrior to express that there is nothing more beautiful than depth of character. The thoughts in this poem come from the values I have been taught and the observations I have made.

16. A Note to Myself

Take a pile of all your accomplishments and set it to fire
In a tornado of vanity, come out as a survivor
When money pours down like rain, run towards a shelter
Let hard work be your ruler and convenience just an advisor
Pull the rope of destiny with all your might
Without expecting it to reach your side
And when life bargains you power, politely decline the offer

If love and lovers were a colour - they would be red for me. This faceless woman is a naive soul, an all committing individual, a raw being, she is forever young and red! This poem brings together various symbols of love- red and ravishing interpreted across the evolving stages of a love story.

17. Love is Red

Long for them from
The very bottom of your heart
Let that feeling enchant you,
Your love should be sweet like strawberries,
Watermelons and apples
Once you digest this love,
Look at them as if they are
As rare as a red picturesque sky
Love them passionately,
Like an aggressive and dominating
Blazing red fire
Appreciate their beauty
Like a florist appreciates
Each and every petal of a rose
With every passing year
Tell them that they have aged like red wine
And then you will realize
Why the poets say
That love is red

18. A Canvas of Thoughts

A thought
Buried deep inside a feeling filled heart
That takes color
Not just in the colours and the construction on the canvas
But in the brazenness of the brushstroke
The confusion/ coordination in the colours
Most importantly
In the eyes of the beholder
The brush and the paint are malleable
They surrender to the artists
To imagination
To mood
To skill
ignorant of the real world events
Helpless in fact useless in isolation
But together
Creating not just a compelling composition.
But evidence..
Of imagination
Of mood
Of skill
Of real world events
A painting is a moment that magically turns into a legacy.

19. Fading in the Shadows

We were digging up the ground to find our treasure
We put in the labour, we waited patiently
With our tools that were dormant sentinels
For our intent was strong but latent

But you gave up, just when we were a tad short of hitting our mark
This was the first test of your affection for me

And when our crown shattered into innumerable pieces
I tried to piece them together with glue
But you sprinted
Because the glass could prick your feet

Slipping through my fingers
But deep in my mind
Slowly, escaping your heart
But never leaving my memory

Death takes colour away from those who get left behind. The darkness is dominant in the early stages of grief which is what is depicted in this painting. A woman staring into nothingness, a woman consumed by nothingness too. A woman trapped in a zone which is dark both within and around. She is not who she used to be. She feels she will never be. She reminisces the gifts that her loved one left behind. Even those gifts will never be the same.

20. The Gift of Death

I would buy you roses on your birthday
Now I leave a bouquet of flowers where you lie
We used to play hide and seek
Now I hide from the way I feel, and seek solace
I remember lying down on my balcony with you
You would look up at the distant stars
But my star was right next to me
Until you too become that elusive star.
You bought me a watch on my birthday
I let out enthusiastic cries of joy
But that watch is now irrelevant
For time just stands still
My birthday is not what it used to be
It's a different date
For a different me
In a different world

This painting and poem capture the lifelong pursuit towards perfection and progress. This painting also celebrates the important yet underrated power of a pause. The woman has covered multiple miles and ups and downs and at dusk she stops herself just for a moment to do the one thing that defines life itself - to breathe!

The poem highlights the unfailing trap of societal norms that push individuals to high standards of achievement with little regard to the joyfulness of life.

21. Pointless Pursuits

There is so much to do in life
So much to choose from
So much to work for
So much to stay away from
And it starts nearly after the beginning ..
A child is welcomed with smiles
But spoken to with instructions
Of right and wrong
Good and bad
Conceptually all beings would then be similar
Except they are not
They are right or wrong
Good or bad
they cannot settle with those labels
The good have to be the best
The bad have to be better
The boundaries become fluid between constant
improvement and ongoing pressure
If only just being was good enough
If only just seeking was rewarded
If only finding love was the epitome of success
For there is no right or wrong
Good or bad , less or more
in the matters of the heart, soul and mind

22. Right on Centre

I often think how it's so easy to determine the mid point of a segmented line
Some come and tell me they are right while some say left is just fine
The right is always right they often say
For all the talk of inclusiveness, the left too wants things done exactly their way
There is always a strong point of view
And a stronger narrative supporting the loud few
I'm constantly being told to pick a side
Being told to defend statements with a thick hide
Why can't the majority which is so silent
Pick the middle instead of being seen as pliant
The problem I think lies in the constant shift
In what is left and what is right
The middle does also have to move constantly doesn't it
That I think is the reason why so many find it tough to fit

23. The Power of You

When you were around
The sun shone brighter
The flowers had more colour
The winds felt cool
The cold invited warmth

When you were around
The mind felt secure
The heart felt nourished
The soul was at peace

When you were around
Every day had stories I could share
Every dream felt real and
Reality felt like a dream

When you were around
It was about us and not me
It was about living in the present
And sculpting a shared vision for the future
Decades of togetherness
Ended in a single moment
It was your heart that stopped beating
And it is mine that doesn't beat the same way anymore

When you left
You took from me joy, colour and calm
For a while

For longer than a while actually
Until I realised
You may have left the world
But you have not , you can not
Leave me.

24. The *Faultless* Diamond

In a secluded township in Africa
Guarded by armed guerrillas
Innumerable slaves spent countless hours
Digging the earth up
Sweating, toiling
Bereft of the right to complain
Denied the thought of making a choice
All they could do, rather, had to do
Was keep searching for me

They worked with dirty hands and rudimentary tools
With no access to clean drinking water
Sanitation or nutritious food
And once they found me, they received no reward or respite
They were compelled to depart from their town
They endured forced relocation and displacement
The earth they dug was no longer theirs

Then I was taken to the processing industries
The diminutive hands of adolescents worked on me
These young ones were denied schooling and education
And were forcibly made to provide labor
During the years meant for dreams and joy
These kids were left feeling despondent and helpless
During the years they should have tired themselves by playing
These children had to slog incessantly

On the outside, I am the pride of Africa
But internally, I carry sinister stories of exploitation
Lives lost, taken, and troubled
To create a flawless shine
I traveled over hundreds of miles
Wiping away thousands of smiles
To find a place of pride
On the crowns of the selfish emperors
Rights were exploited, I was cut and chiseled
And finally, I was transformed from a mere rough rock
To a "faultless" diamond.

9 789359 894461

Printed at Repro India Ltd.